# DORKING
## & THE MOLE VALLEY
### PAST & PRESENT

# DORKING
## & THE MOLE VALLEY
### PAST & PRESENT

IAN WILLIAMS
& CAPEL CAMERA CLUB

The History Press

The History Press
The Mill • Brimscombe Port • Stroud •
Gloucestershire • GL5 2QG

First published 2008

Reprinted 2010, 2012, 2013

Copyright © Ian Williams, 2008

*Title page photograph*: An aerial view of
Dorking looking towards the old town
station.

British Library Cataloguing in Publication Data
A catalogue record for this book is available from the
British Library.

ISBN 978-07509-4582-0

Typeset in 10.5/13.5 Photina.
Typesetting and origination by
The History Press.
Printed and bound in Great Britain by
Marston Book Services Limited, Didcot

*Dedicated to the memory of William (Bill) Williams,*
*father of the author*
*28 October 1928 – 24 November 2007*

The London Scottish Regiment on parade for training in Dorking at the bottom of Ansell
Road.

# CONTENTS

The bridge at Brockham looking south towards the Green.

Coldharbour Lane, Dorking.

# INTRODUCTION

The Surrey Hills in and around Dorking offer some of the most spectacular scenery in England. Add to this some of the most picturesque villages in the south, like Brockham, Betchworth and Ockley, whose beauty have graced many a postcard, chocolate box or jigsaw over the years, and you know you live in an area of outstanding beauty.

I was born in Dorking General Hospital over forty years ago and have, for the best part of my life, lived in the area. I have collected picture postcards for over twenty years and currently live in the village of Brockham with my wife, two daughters and son. During this time I have amassed an enviable collection extending to well over 5,000 cards; but it is stored for safe-keeping and only available for viewing on special occasions. This is one of the major reasons that this book has been compiled and printed, to enable other people to share and fully appreciate the beauty and extent of this fine collection.

The collection started in the mid-1980s after a visit to a local flower show. Walking around the grounds, I came across a bric-a-brac stall. Hidden away in a shoe box was a selection of postcards of the area. The top card was a view I recognised – Brockham Bridge. Belonging to the local fishing club, who met on the bridge before each competition, I avidly purchased the card for £1. As I walked from the stall, the lady serving offered the balance of cards for a further £3 – but I declined. In hindsight this was possibly not the best move I have ever made, bearing in mind that I have individual cards in my collection valued at over £75.

I regularly contribute to Dorking's input to the national heritage weekends in September each year. My fine display of picture postcards of Dorking and district can be viewed in Mole Valley's Council Office and now extends to eighteen boards. Over the years this display has been viewed by many hundreds of people. At this event a couple of years ago, an elderly couple were overheard arguing over the precise location now of a picture on display. This provoked the idea for a 'then and now' scenario.

Just before Christmas in 2005 I visited Denbies Vineyard in Dorking to view a display of photographs by Capel Camera Club. So impressed was I by this display that when the offer of publishing this title was made I immediately approached the club to contribute the 'now' selection of illustrations. The club, which operates to extremely high standards, offers the opportunity for photographers of all standards to learn the magic of photography by competing at an equal level to near professional standard amateurs. I would like to thank them for their valuable contribution to this title.

# CAPEL CAMERA CLUB
# CONTRIBUTORS

### ROBERT G. ARTHUR, ARPS

Bob has had a lifelong interest in photography and is a member of the Royal Photographic Society, gaining their distinctions of LRPS in 1990 and then the ARPS in 1996. Despite the massive move to digital technology by the general public and most professional photographers, Bob has continued to use the traditional wet darkroom for all his monochrome work, which is still his preferred medium. His main interests are studio portraiture, people, documentary and creative-style printing in monochrome. He is currently an active member of Dorking Camera Club and the Chairman of Capel Camera Club. His work has featured over the years in magazines and the occasional photographic year book.

### DUNCAN JENNINGS C. ENG, LRPS

Retired civil engineer Duncan lives in Capel and has an interest and passion for photography stretching back to his schooldays. He studied photography at Guildford Adult Education Institute and has gained the first distinction of the Royal Photographic Society. His main interests and sources of photographs these days are portraiture, worldwide travel and local history. Duncan greatly enjoys the restoration of old photos and has previously assisted in supplying restored pictures for publication. Of his four children, two are professionally engaged in photography, one writing for photo journals and the other working for a leading picture bank selling to newspapers and magazines. Duncan regularly has his work accepted and shown in national exhibitions and uses traditional film and modern digital cameras.

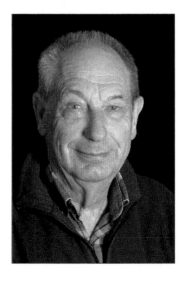

### MAURICE BOOTH, ARPS

Maurice bought his first 'proper' camera, an elderly folding camera, in 1948 and soon began to develop and print his own black and white photographs. He joined the Reigate Photographic Society and later Croydon Photographic Club. Membership of the Royal Photographic Society followed and he gained the distinction of ARPS in 1967. Maurice joined the Capel Camera Club in 1965, and became their president for twenty years. Now in his eighties, he is still very busy with Capel Club and enters many exhibitions and competitions.

### MICK MANSBRIDGE

Mick first became interested in photography about fifteen years ago and joined the Capel Camera Club in order to better understand the ins and outs of the subject. Since then he has gone on to win a number of trophies for competitions within the club and in various other local events. He has a major interest in water pictures and has sold a number of framed copies of his work at club exhibitions held locally.

### BRIAN ROBSON, DPAGB (deceased)

Brian's interest in photography started when he was a teenager taking photos of his family holidays. As his interest progressed he built a darkroom in the bathroom from where he produced black and white prints. But it wasn't until 1990 when he gave up playing cricket and hockey, needing a less physical hobby, that his true passion for photography developed. After retiring from a career as an accountant he was able to travel extensively, enjoying and capturing memorable images of stunning parts of the USA, Africa and Australia. But his favourite place to take pictures remained Northumberland. In 2003 he was awarded a distinction in slides from the Photographic Alliance of Great Britain and until his sudden death in December 2006, was chairman of the Surrey Photographic Association.

# 1

# *Dorking Central*

A classic view of South Street, which apart from the increased levels of traffic, has changed very little in over 100 years. The building to the left of the picture was, until 2006, a showroom for F.W. Mays & Co., a car dealership and garage which had associations with the town for a great many years. Although there are over 100 years between each of the photographs, the faithful old cedar tree still stands today. I have fond memories of the local bus garage which stood behind where this picture was taken and also of the Queen's Head public house, next to which stood a legendary transport café and local shop. Just walking past this shop, which is now a takeaway pizza establishment, brings back memories of Jamboree bags, Black Jacks and Fruit Salad sweets.

The Wesleyan Church in South Street, with its fine Gothic revival style spire rising to over 90ft, was sadly demolished in the early 1970s to make way for the modern offices that currently adorn the site. Methodist minister John Wesley first visited Dorking on 12 January 1764, the first of nineteen visits over the next twenty-two years. The building to the right-hand side of the church was a barn in which animals were held before slaughter at the local abattoir, which was located to the rear of the Bull's Head. I have vivid memories of these poor creatures being driven down the road to their doom. Meat from the abattoir was sold at the local butchers who were based next door to the Bull's Head. As the slaughtering of animals became more regulated, the abattoir closed down in the late 1980s. The abattoir itself has now been converted to residential homes.

The South Street offices of Dorking Urban District Council were also the home of the town's post office until it moved to its current position in 1932. As can be seen from this the old image dating back to 1913, South Street was once a narrow lane such as West Street remains. It was widened to accommodate the war memorial and now abandoned bandstand in 1919. The entrance to the famous South Street caves, where I am one of the team of voluntary guides, is accessed through a small door to the left of the war memorial, which is just visible on the extreme right of the modern view. Before the widening, the caves would have been accessed through a door in the back garden of in the cottage in the centre right of the old photograph.

In the days of horse-drawn coach travel between London and the south coast, the Bull's Head was a recognised point for the changing of horses en route. It also offered the opportunity for weary travellers to take a break from their trip to London or from the seaside. Providing board and lodging, the inn was very popular with travelling salesmen at the turn of the century. Today the public house remains remarkably unchanged and is still a very popular venue with Dorking people. It has a fine display of antique prints of the town adorning its walls.

The junction of High Street, South Street and West Street creates a focal point in the town commonly known as Pump Corner, because of the communal water pump located there. When people say to me how much the town has changed over the years I suggest they turn their eyes skyward, because by comparing the old and modern pictures of the High Street we can clearly see that the upper storeys of the buildings have changed very little.

Dorking is well-documented as a market town and the livestock market was held weekly in the High Street outside the White Horse Hotel until 1926 when it moved to a purpose-built area behind the buildings opposite the hotel. The livestock market sadly disappeared in the 1960s, although the weekly traders' market continues. In the early 1980s when today's St Martin's Walk Shopping Mall was constructed, a number of graves were discovered just outside the walls of the cemetery of St Martin's Church.

The White Horse Hotel with its central location has been the place of residence for many famous visitors to the town. It is an outstanding building with its gabled roof and an interior frame with oak beams dating back well over 400 years. Charles Dickens is reputed to have stayed in the town when writing *The Pickwick Papers*, and allegedly based a number of characters from the book on people he met during his stay. The most famous of these was a coachman called William Broad, on whom he allegedly based his character, Tony Weller.

HIGH STREET, DORKING

The Surrey Yeoman, originally named the Royal Oak, is another public house with a long history in the town and at one point it was the last building in the High Street. The Surrey Yeomanry also has a long and distinguished history connected with the town – the last Earl of Rothes being the colonel of the regiment. Our modern picture shows just how much the north side of the High Street has been developed over the past ten years with the fine old tree being replaced by a short terrace of shops.

The High Street, Dorking

The Ram Inn was demolished in 1959 to make way for the current rank of shops. It derived its name from Ram Alley which we all now know as Dene Street. Before the development of the A24 Dorking bypass between 1931 and 1934, Ram Alley was one of the two major routes south from the town, the other being the now-named Horsham Road, which was a turnpike with its own toll gate located at Garth House halfway up the hill to North Holmwood. Just out of sight in our old view is the local confectioner's called Weller's. The shop has moved and downsized in recent years, but was once heaven for local youngsters like myself on pocket money day, as it had the best local supply of jarred sweets in the town.

S 17213 - High Street East, Dorking

In the 1940s, London Road (the road to the right of the picture) was the main route to and from London, and therefore this junction was very busy and important. Its importance is further illustrated by the fact that despite the apparent lack of cars, a policeman still stands in the central reservation to direct traffic. The policeman has today been replaced by the all familiar traffic lights. It is also worth noting that to the extreme left of the picture, a garage is still located today – nearly seventy years after the original photograph was taken.

Within my lifetime the Public Hall in West Street was used by the local fire brigade and on the opposite page is a picture postcard which was posted in 1913 showing the voluntary local fire brigade testing out new equipment on the site. The volunteer fire brigade was formed in 1870 and had a call-out strength of six officers and seventeen men equipped with a manual escape (being demonstrated picture opposite) and two steam pumps. Over the years the building has served the town well, having been a cinema, a library and meeting house for both public and religious meetings. Miss Cotton, the daughter of Sir Arthur Cotton, both keen supporters of Evangelical and Temperance work in the town, held gospel meetings on Sunday evenings in the rooms above the hall. These attracted a great following, so William Dinnage recollects in his writings published in the *Dorking Advertiser* in the summer of 1963.

This view has changed little in nearly 100 years as West Street is still the main route into the town from Westcott and Guildford. The Old Public Hall, which was built in about 1871, still dominates the picture with its ornate frontage. To the right can be seen the old stonemason's yard and just out of shot is Clarendon House, which was for a number of years a mathematical and commercial school for boys.

# 2

# *Dorking Back Streets*

 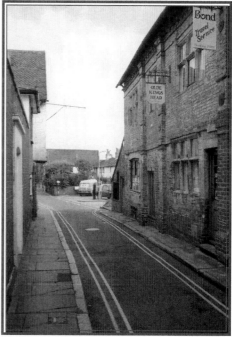

The view as you enter North Street from is junction with Pump Corner has changed very little in 100 years. The Old King's Head hostelry is no longer in operation, but in its courtyard to the rear, is a thriving commercial square of small retail outlets. According to the recollections of Charles Rose in the book *Memories of Old Dorking*, the public house has many stories linked with it, not least a macabre wake held for an Irishman in the mid-nineteenth century. The man worked at the chalk pits above the town and met with an unfortunate accident. There not being enough money available to his colleagues and countrymen to provide a funeral, assistance was sought from a wealthy local lady. The funds were provided on the strict understanding that no rite of any kind should be undertaken. And so it was in the deep of night, so as not to be caught, the mourners lifted the deceased from his coffin and sat him on a stool at a table in the public house with a drink in front of him. One after another they chanted at him, 'O' Willie, why did ye go and leave all these good things behind you?' The rite did not bring poor Willie back to life, and in fear of this breach of confidence the mourners are alleged to have left the town, never to return.

Archway Place is a tiny back alley linking North Street with Portland Road, so why someone would publish a picture postcard of it is a mystery as it is of little historic interest. However, behind the hedge in the modern picture is now located Meadow Bank football ground, home of Dorking FC – the Chicks. The team was formed in 1880 and was the second-oldest club in Surrey. Before the club's move to the current ground in 1953, they played at the pitches in Pixham Lane. It was from here that they carved their early success at both junior and senior levels. In the 1907/8 season the team, which included three members of the Fuller family, were winners of the Mid-Surrey League and runners-up in the Surrey Charity Cup.

This view of one of the two small back alleys off the western end of the High Street is of interest for a couple of reasons. At the right-hand side of the entrance today stand the premises of Bookends, the discount book store, which was until about forty years ago another of Dorking's many now-vanished pubs, the Wheat Sheaf. The cellar is occasionally opened to the public (usually during the national heritage weekends in September) for people to view the cock-fighting pit in its basement, which is carved out of the sandstone and represents the last locally known venue for the barbaric sport. The second reason is that the postcard we have on display is a second edition print. The first print contained the picture of an old man standing under the light to the right of the picture, copies of which are now extremely rare.

A bit of old Dorking.

This view of Mill Lane is still recognisable, but has changed a number of times since the original picture was taken. Mill Lane, leading to Meadow Bank and Dorking's Mill Pond, was once the home of a number of thriving businesses including a tannery owned by Mr Blaker and Boxall's brewery. The Pipbrook at the bottom of the lane was a resource that was extremely well used by local businesses, as aside from the mills, local breweries and tanneries flourished along its banks.

This is a slightly misleading postcard as Church Street Cottages were actually located in Meadowbrook Road. It is true that the view was most probably taken while standing in Church Street, so the publisher can be forgiven. The cottages, even at the turn of the twentieth century, looked run-down and were demolished by the Urban District Council in 1936 after receiving slum clearance orders. During 1936, 81 premises in the town were demolished as unsanitary and 217 people were rehoused in recently built properties in Fraser Gardens, Dorking and Watson Road, Westcott.

The picturesque Victorian arch adjoining Rose Hill House was, at the time of its construction, a private entrance to the rear of the property. Today it is the exit from Sainsbury's car park for vehicles of the appropriate height – although in recent years others have attempted to exit this way with serious consequences. To the right of the modern view is a small development of townhouses which were built on the site of the slaughter pens of Chitty's Butchers, located next door to the Bull's Head which is just visible in the background under the arch.

The Horsham road was, until the construction of Dorking bypass, the main route south out of Dorking for travellers visiting Horsham and the south coast. The other route was along Ram Alley and onwards to Chart Lane. Both routes took you across Holmwood Common, which was notorious for its highwaymen and thieves. In days of horse-drawn coach travel, Horsham road was a turnpike with a toll gate located to the south of the site of this picture, almost opposite the Bush public house at Garth House. To the right of the picture in the middle background are the steep steps leading up to Dorking Hospital. There is still a hospital on the site, but on a very limited scale, with the majority of the site now developed into housing.

Pipbrook Mill, also known as Patching Mill or Dorking Mill, occupies the site of an eleventh-century mill, and its mill pond is recorded in the manorial survey map of 1649. Today the mill pond is a much-loved feature of the park known locally as Meadow Bank recreation ground. The mill itself has not operated commercially since 1932, and is now the business premises of a local publishing company. Since the original picture was taken the mill rush has been dammed at its western end causing the rush to be reduced to no more than a small babbling stream.

This view from the top of Cotmandene on initial inspection has changed very little, but look deeper and you will notice that what were once fields to the right background has now been developed into large houses. Dorking's annual horse and fatstock fair was held on Ascension Day each year and supplemented by a fairground, which was originally sited on Butter High and South Street. However, owing to increased traffic in the town it was moved to Cotmandene, where even today the fair still pays a visit around that time of year. Cotmandene was also the location of Dorking's first cricket ground, where in the eighteenth century two-day matches were held, attracting thousands of spectators from the surrounding area.

A fine view of Dene Street, or Ram Alley as it was formerly named, photographed in about 1900. The building to the left of the picture is the White Hart public house, while on the opposite side of the road is Constable Court. This fine listed building has been tastefully restored by local solicitors Downs for use as offices and a self-contained flat. The history of this legal firm can be traced back to 1855, when it first started operating in Dorking High Street as Down, Scott & Down. In recent times it has grown dramatically, incorporating a number of small local operations within the organisation, but has still retained a strong commercial base in the town.

Falkland Arms, Dorking. Terminus for London Busses

The junction of Hampstead Road and Falkland Road was, at the turn of the century, the terminus for London buses, bringing day trippers to the town. Visitors would refresh themselves at the Falkland Arms or the Prince of Wales, which is a few yards behind the camera, before continuing their trip on foot to one of the many local attractions. These would have included Milton Heath, Ranmore and, of course, Leith Hill Tower. The terminus moved to a purpose-built garage located at the junction of South Street and Horsham Road, but sadly this to has now been developed into housing, owing to the declining use of public transport.

The old vicarage of St Martin's stands on the junction of Vincent Lane and Westcott Road, within the boundary of old Sondes Place House. The previous vicarage was situated in Back Lane, now Church Street, but this was abandoned in 1800 because of its poor condition. The property in Westcott Road was utilised as a vicarage until 1986 when the vicar moved into the property's modernised stable block and the house was converted into apartments. While the building today is still recognisable as the one pictured in the postcard, it has lost a certain amount of its seventeenth-century splendour and charm.

# 3

# *Dorking Outskirts*

As St Martin's churchyard approached saturation by the mid-1850s, the new cemetery, located on the Reigate road, was opened on 21 November 1855, offering 4 acres of consecrated ground. At its entrance is still an ornate gatehouse leading through to two chapels. To the right of the gatehouse as you enter the site there was also a mortuary. The site was extended by another 5 acres in 1889, and a further 3 acres were added in 1923. The east chapel is opened on national heritage weekends each September, offering the general public an insight to its history and even a guided tours of some of the more interesting and famous graves.

Dorking, Punch Bowl Inn.

The Punch Bowl Inn was built by Sir John Soane and dates back to 1780. It is located on the main road between Reigate and Dorking has offered many numbers of travellers the opportunity to refresh themselves before arriving at Dorking. The modern image shows the inn today as a fast food restaurant and flourishing motel, which was redeveloped in 1971. As this book is put to bed, the site is again changing and the fast food restaurant is being demolished for further redevelopment.

Dorking. Punch Bowl Lane.

The tranquil Punch Bowl Lane runs from the Reigate Road through to Chart Lane. Roughly 500yds up the road to the right was the East Lodge entrance to Deepdene House. The access road known as Lady Gate, allowed visitors to experience fine views across the estates, which was then open parkland towards Dorking and Ranmore. Today much of the area has been developed with large private residential dwellings.

The current Castle Mill stands on a site which was recorded in the Domesday Book. The mill had fierce local competition, but was the last of the local mills to close in 1952. Much discussion was entered into by the Dorking Urban District Council about how to preserve the property, and in the end, permission was granted to turn it into a residence. Restoration of the property was undertaken by Michael Manser and his work earned a European Heritage Award in 1974. In more recent times the old weir has been demolished by the water authority and a new one installed, dropping the water levels by over 5ft in an effort to better control floods. In our modern view the mill building is sadly obscured by trees.

Located just above Castle Mill on the Reigate Road, this hostelry has, over the years, been home to a public house, a restaurant, a café and a nightclub. Today it has returned to its former use as a popular public house/restaurant. Above can be seen a walled area with tiled top, behind which was a swimming pool. After the closure of the Station Road public baths in June 1939 owing to leakage, this became Dorking's only swimming pool. The open-air pool had a high diving platform at its north end, as can be seen from the old picture above. It sadly closed in the 1950s also owing to an undetectable leak, and now forms part of the car park.

Our old image shows the steep and narrow track which led from the main Reigate Road down to Castle Mill. One can imagine a horse-drawn cart, heavily laden with corn to be milled, edging its way down here. To the right-hand side of the road is Betchworth Park with its chestnut grove and open parkland extending into Brockham village. In 1927 a new bridge over the River Mole was constructed (to the east of this picture) and the road was improved by widening it and resurfacing with tarmac. Today the A25 is extremely busy and the old view is almost unrecognisable.

The Westcott Road in Dorking at its Milton Heath end has changed very little in nearly 100 years. In its glory years this approach to the town boasted a fine avenue of trees, which were very sadly devastated in the huge storms of October 1987. Adrian White, an eminent local businessman and owner of the Denbies Estate, made a generous donation allowing the replanting of trees to ensure the road was restored to its former glory for future generations. In the middle background is one of two entrances to Bury Hill, the mansion home of the Barclay family. The eighteenth-century mansion was turned over to the military in 1940 for use in the war effort. After the war, the building was sold for conversion into apartments. Sadly during October 1949 a fire broke out destroying much of the central part of the mansion. After the owner, Colonel Barclay died, the rest of the estate was sold in lots in 1952 to cover death duties. Today Bury Hill is known countrywide for its coarse fishing in a beautifully landscaped four-lake complex.

Pixham Lane, Dorking.

Although today Pixham Lane is much wider, it is still easily recognisable from the old picture. Most of the properties have changed very little externally over the last century with nothing more than the addition of television aerials. In the middle background we can make out the Lutyens-designed church and beyond that the general store at the junction with Leslie Road. The church which was erected in 1903 and replaced the iron room, a forbidding place of worship, which was cold in the winter and roasting in the summer.

When the Shrub Hill estate was sold in 1881, a local man, Mr Butcher, purchased an area of land off of Pixham Lane, which he developed into two plots of forty to fifty houses. Today these make up Leslie Road and Riverside. Our old picture shows a small handcart with lettering on the side stating 'A. Butcher & Son', most probably belonging to a local baker of that name. Whether this is anything to do with the developer I am unsure, but it is not beyond the realms of possibility as initially the development was rented and it would have been the landlord's responsibility to maintain the properties. Today the road retains much of its charm and there is a fine walk between here and Castle Mill, which starts at the eastern end of the road.

The Station, Dorking.

Our old picture depicts a typical approach to a town station, with a railway inn (The Star & Garter) to the right, and on the left behind the fence was the goods yard and engine shed. At the bottom end of the approach road was a builders' merchant which disappeared in the 1980s when the site was redeveloped into modern offices. In the 1960s and '70s outside the station was a transport café, which served cooked breakfasts and hot beverages to the taxi drivers operating the rank. Today the public house/hotel is called the Lincoln Arms, the old station has been redeveloped into modern offices and the goods yard is a huge British Rail car park.

Dorking has three railway stations. Dorking North is on the main line, servicing traffic on the Horsham to London routes. This is the station in the background of the view on the previous page. The other two are on the Redhill to Guildford line, which runs over the bridges on this page: Dorking Town, which is now called Dorking West, and Deepdene (formerly known as Boxhill station) which is located to the left of the bridge in both pictures. The quaint old brick bridge was demolished in 1964 as the A24 was widened to become a dual carriageway to accommodate the huge increase in traffic. By 1969 the station building had been demolished. Today the station is unmanned with nothing more than a little shelter on either platform, but it is good to see that the fine gable-fronted house is still in existence.

Cliftonville is a small development to the eastern side of the Horsham road, opposite its junction with Hampstead Road. The collection of houses was erected in the 1880s and derives its name from the developer Joseph Clift, a chemist in the High Street and member of the local board. Built for occupation by the middle classes, Cliftonville represents some fine examples of architecture of the time. Today the view has changed little, save for the addition of motor cars to the scene.

# 4

# *Brockham, Betchworth & Buckland*

Brockham's Borough Bridge lies to the north of the village. This single carriageway crossing the River Mole was built in 1737 by Richard and Thomas Skilton, local surveyors. In 1991 it was strengthened by Surrey County Council to bring it up to modern standards because of the increased flow of traffic across its spans. At the same time the arched footbridge was added for improved pedestrian access. The field to the left of the old picture was put up for development for housing in the 1930s, but the proposed project failed after potential buyers were warned by locals of the severe danger of flooding.

Oakdene Road, Brockham Green.

It is said by local folk that everyone in the village has at some time lived in or had relatives living in Oakdene Road. Oakdene was developed during the late Victorian era with the white cottages to the right of our old picture representing some of the first houses in the street – Sunnyside Villas being built in 1907. Further housing was built in the late 1940s consisting of council houses with two or three bedrooms. Until the construction in the 1950s of the bridge across the stream which lies halfway down the road, vehicle access was via Wheelers Lane only.

Brockham Green

The view north across the Green from the church towards the Duke's Head public house remains as tranquil today as it did 100 years ago. Cricket used to be played here on summer weekends up until the 1970s when the club moved to its new purpose-built clubhouse in Middle Street. I have fond memories as a lad of being taken to the Green on a sunny afternoon to watch the cricket while my parents had a drink at one of the two hostelries there. A bottle of coke with two straws and a packet of cheese and onion crisps completed the treat. Although cricket is no longer played here, I still get a great deal of pleasure taking my young family down to the Green for refreshments during summer weekends.

Middle Street in Brockham has seen a great deal of development over the past twenty years. The grassy meadow which lay to the north of this terrace of Victorian cottages was developed into Middle Green. Building work started in 1989 and the first residents moved in during July 1992. Opposite the houses, the fields were turned over to the trustees of the cricket club and developed into the area locally known now as the Rec. With cricket and football pitches, a brick-built clubhouse and a children's playground, it is now the centre of focus for a vast majority of the village's sports teams. Middle Street is today a very busy road and was the site of a pilot for a community speedwatch initiative which has now been adopted across much of Surrey.

The Saxon church (rebuilt) of St Michaels in Betchworth, with its Norman additions. This old view was published by C. Harman, a local trader and part of a large family associated with the area. His pictures are very distinctive and usually include members of his eight-strong young family. Our view of the church from its northern aspect clearly shows its fine lychgate and bell tower with clock. From my home in Brockham you can hear the welcoming bells calling parishioners to their worship at about 10.30 a.m. most Sundays.

Another Harman view, this time of Betchworth's bridge across the River Mole. As was so typical of this local publisher, some of his family are featured in the shot. Harman was related to William Harman, who with his young wife, ran Brockham's bakery and general store which was located in the the building now named Surrey House, which stands to the north of the village club. Just over the bridge on the north-eastern side, lies an orchard in which is located a pit (now semi-filled with silt) which was used by a local farmer for dipping sheep. My father recalled standing on the bridge to watch this event on a number of occasions as a young lad. Today the orchard is untended and only occasionally visited by anglers.

The Dolphin was one of three public houses located in the parish at the turn of the twentieth century and today is sadly the only one remaining. It is reputed to have been one of the last public houses in Surrey to brew its own beer and cider, which ceased in 1926 owing to increasing regulations and expenses. The Bridger family were associated with the Dolphin from 1862 until 1930, Frank Bridger Snr being the landlord until his death in 1900 and his son Frank Jnr following in his father's footsteps. Frank Jnr was a keen angler and formed the Dolphin Angling Club. Until the sale of the pub in 1930, on the wall above the bar, hung a glass-encased stuffed pike which Frank Jnr. is reputed to have caught from the river in the orchard below the pub.

The original hostelry of this name stood to the south-east of the one pictured in our old shot. The new premises were built following the construction of the new A25 in 1927, which saw a rapid decline in passing trade. The new Barley Mow was run by mother-and-son team Elizabeth and Percy Burnham until Elizabeth's death in 1937 at the age of 61. In November 1940, a string of German bombs was dropped in the parish, the first landing close to the pub, in a line until the last landed in Brockham Warren on the side of Boxhill; the pub was severely damaged. Damage was repaired and the business flourished until the 1970s, when it changed its name to the Arkle Manor. Today, after several refurbishments, the premises is a pub/restaurant favoured by families.

Buckland village store and post office has been in the same location since at least 1838 and has over the years been a key feature of many photographs and paintings of the village. The structure of fifteenth-century origin with seventeenth-century extensions is originally thought to have been an inn called the Leg of Mutton and Cauliflower. The property also has strong links with horse-drawn coach travel, for just outside the shop, 8ft from the ground, is the old letterbox in which coachmen could deposit mail without dismounting. Today it is still a flourishing business which retains the majority of its previous charm.

The view across the village pond to the Green really is a chocolate-box type picture, and few could imagine that today, just behind the camera, the main A25 runs with huge amount of daily traffic. The towered barn to the left of the picture was converted to a residential dwelling in 1981 and 1982 with little change to the frontal elevation. The barn's history includes being used as a temporary church between 1861 and 1862 while St Mary's was being rebuilt. The local myth is that the tower was constructed to make it more church-like; however, this is not true as it was already an integral part of the property, housing a massive lead-lined water tank which supplied the whole village. During conversion of the property over a ton of lead was removed from the tank. This view's most recent claim to fame is being featured on the cover of the 1997 local Ordnance Survey map.

Arterial Road from Reigate Heath, Reigate

Named 'Arterial Road' in our old image, this view actually depicts the new A25 from the top of Buckland looking west towards Betchworth lime works – which can be made out in the distance. It is believed that the garage was built at roughly the same time as the road (1927) as it is shown on the 1934 Ordnance Survey map as 'Fisher's Garage'. Today the site is a Shell filling station, with a brisk trade on this busy stretch of the A25. To the middle left of the picture is a wooded area which shields the old view from showing Broome Park and Hall.

Situated close to the western edge of the parish of Buckland, the Red Lion is often understandably mistakenly thought to be a Betchworth inn. The inn has strong sporting associations, for in 1935 the owner was recorded as Major R.G. Thompson, an old Cambridge soccer blue. The venue boasted a squash court, quoits (a game like hoopla played with metal rings) and Buckland cricket field was to the rear – home of the Surrey Sevens Cricket Club. Cricket is today still played behind the pub, but sadly the squash court was converted into bedrooms to offer bed and breakfast facilities for visitors.

# 5

# *Leigh & Newdigate*

Another inn on the green, this seventeenth-century public house has played many roles in the heart of village life. For instance at one time, as the village had no butcher, the landlord had a travelling wagon from which he would sell fresh meat to the parishioners on a weekly basis. Being located adjacent to the church, the Plough has also seen many visitors through its doors before weddings, after funerals and of course after the Sunday service. It also has an association with the now-banned sport of fox hunting and I have recollections of the hunt meeting outside the venue with smartly dressed red-jacketed riders and a pack of baying hounds.

Our old view shows Leigh forge in about 1907. It was occupied at the time by George Flint. His son Frank took over the forge in 1910 after George passed away, and very soon turned it into a petrol station and garage which did a strong trade. Between 1929 and 1953 he also ran a highly successful taxi firm from the premises. Today the site has been developed into residential dwellings; the two houses at the forefront being aptly named The Smithy and The Barn.

The village store and post office adjoined Chantry Cottage which boasts two remaining bays of a medieval building and could possibly has been an ecclesiastical building. The shop was run from the late 1930s by Miss Gurney, but closed in 1953 and a new post office was opened in Dawes Green. A new shop also opened to cover demand, and this was located in Clayhill Road. Today the view is almost unrecognisable, being obstructed by trees and shrubs planted to give the homeowners some privacy. The only remaining business on the Green in 2007 is the Plough. The village even shares its vicar with neighbouring Brockham.

Our postcard view shows the old Leigh school and pump with children playing on the green outside the Plough. The well was dug on the green in 1875 and soon after capped with a pump for use by villagers. The old school was built in about 1846 and enlarged in 1884 to cater for the growing demand for education among the working classes. Late Victorian times saw the village grow quickly and by 1919 a new school offering three large classrooms, a hall and playing field opened halfway along Tapners Road, which today remains the site of the village school.

The Six Bells is a charming little public house situated opposite St Peter's Church on the main road through the village. When the pub opened in about 1784, it was known as the Five Bells or just the Bells; it changed its name after the church had an additional bell hung in 1803. Around the same time the landlord, Mr Cheesman, also supplied the Duke of Norfolk's household with ale. The last manorial court of the Manor of Cudworth was held at the Six Bells in 1908. The car featured in our old view could well be that of Dr Wakefield, who, in 1897, was one of the first people in the area to own one.

Newdigate's fine village hall was built in 1901 as a gift to the village by Mrs Farnell Watson in memory of her husband. It was originally named Newdigate Village Club, and the lettering with this name is still clear in the brickwork above the entrance. By 1924 it was decided to extend the hall and install central heating to cater for its ever-increasing popularity as a meeting place for local groups, clubs and societies. In 1935 a social club was built and licensed to sell alcohol. Mrs Farnell Watson had stipulated that there should never be alcohol served or consumed in the building, and although the new club was a separate building, she is said to have been so upset that she insisted on the memorial stone which she had laid in 1901 being removed.

The village pond was originally a cart pond used to swell the wooden wheels of farm carts so the iron rims fitted securely, but by the time our old photo was taken it was obviously not being put to such practical use. It is located in what the locals call Church Lane which begins opposite the Six Bells, but the road was also known as School Lane; because from 1660 until 1965 it was the site of a sequence of three schools, the last of which was demolished in 1965 when the new modern village school was built in Village Street. Today the pond is maintained on a regular basis by a group of dedicated villagers to stop it getting overgrown and eventually silting up.

Standing on the site of a twelfth-century chapel, St Peter's represents a fine example of a stone- and timber-built church. Its great oak tower which rises to 60ft has three square storeys topped by an octagonal spire and has been dated using dendrochronology (a method of dating trees and timber by the rings present) to 1525. The weight of the spire is supported by four great oak timbers, 18in square, which rest on massive wooden slabs. A specialist craftsman was recruited in 1985 when the tower was renovated to train local men in how to craft and replace the worn outer shingles. The modern view shows the work undertaken over 20 years earlier has ensured St Peter's fine fascia is still available to villagers and visitors today.

# 6

# *Capel, Ockley & Beare Green*

Wolves Hill marks the southern approach to Capel Village, and as can been seen from comparing the old and new views, this has changed quite dramatically in the 100 years that separate the photographs. Coles Lane, the road running left from the junction, was until the construction of the A24 Capel bypass in the early 1980s, the main road linking the village with its neighbour, Ockley. Behind the tall hedge to the right, a number of tasteful modern detached houses have been built, and on the left-hand side of the main road are now the two small estates of Carterdale and Bennetts Wood. The group of buildings in the middle foreground of our old photograph is today a residential house called the Old Dairy, the gardens of which are opened to the public annually and are well worth a visit.

Our old photograph depicts what we believe to be the opening day of Capel Church Hall in about 1911 – locally known as the reading room. The hall, like so many others, was a focal point for village life outside the church and public houses. Everything happened here from whist drives to local dances. The hall was extended further in 1956 with the stone marking the occasion recording its being laid by Waldo Porges Esq. Q.C. on 7 July 1956. This stone also records the chairman at the time being A.R. Carter of the village store and garage. M.E. Markham was treasurer and O.B. Toogood was the honorary secretary. The extension was built by the Dorking firm of Geo. J. Arthur, who are also noted on the memorial stone. Today the hall remains an active part of village life and until 2006 the village pre-school operated from it daily.

Built in 1876 to meet the increasing demand from local Methodists for a place of worship, Capel's Wesleyan Chapel is located at the southern end of The Street, which is the main road through the village. The first minister recorded was Mr Sewell, who had a strong following by the time the chapel was built; he must have been a very busy man as he was also the stationmaster at Ockley to the south-west of the village. Sadly in 2001/2 the church, which had fallen into disrepair, was put up for sale and purchased by a developer. The building has been tastefully converted into two modern homes retaining much of its old charm.

The Quaker movement has a long and happy relationship with Dorking. Dorking's Friends meeting house, located on Butter Hill, is one of eight meeting houses within a 15-mile radius. Capel's Friends meeting house, although not as large as Dorking's, still opens it doors every Sunday at 11 a.m. for all those wishing to attend.

At one time Capel boasted three fine public houses which were all very well attended as they were located on the main route between Dorking, Horsham and the south coast beyond. Capel was also another stopping point for the horse-drawn coach service which ran daily between Dorking, Horsham and Worthing/Brighton with the main inn associated with the change of horses being the King's Head. Our old image shows a fully laden Vanderbilt's coach being hauled by four horses. The Vanderbilt coach was a private venture which ran through Capel between 1910 and 1913. The public house remained a busy venue frequented by passing trade until the building of the Capel bypass in the early 1980s. The bypass, while being a blessing for villagers who lived on the route, proved the beginning of the end for many local businesses, the King's Head included. Today the property has been developed to provide yet more housing for the village, but the main building of the pub is thankfully still recognisable.

A view of the entrance to the northern end of the village in about 1910. The Street, which runs the length of the village, appears to be relatively unmade and used mainly by horse-drawn transport including the famous Vanderbilt coaches operating between Chichester, Horsham and London. Pictured in our old view is what appears to be a tinker's cart, which would have travelled the area selling pots, pans and other household goods, while providing sharpening services for household knives and garden implements. The charming cottages to the right of both pictures have remarkably retained much of their character, apart from the necessity for parking at the front.

The old Capel forge, having fallen into disrepair, was purchased by a Dorking-based paper merchants A. H. James & Co. in the early 1990s. They redeveloped it into modern offices which retained the rustic appearance both internally and externally. In 2002/3 the property was taken over by the local doctors surgery, and still remains in place today. With a bus stop located directly opposite the building today, the forge's position as a reinvented surgery serves it well.

All of the old images from the section on Ockley are from the magnificent work of Percy Lloyd and the first, of the Red Lion, is an extremely fine example. As a film crew would obviously attract a lot of local attention today, so did a travelling man with a camera back in the early twentieth century. Pictured outside the inn are not only a good selection of locals on all forms of transport, but watching over proceedings is the local bobby. The Red Lion's roots date back to the seventeenth century, and when Percy Lloyd was visiting, it boasted the status of a family and commercial hotel with stabling, loose boxes and open and closed carriage hire. Our modern picture didn't attract quite as much attention, but the inn is still family orientated with family dining and a large beer garden.

At the time of our old picture the village postmaster was R.A. Hookey and the double-gabled house with the sloping canopy was the post office and general stores. Postmen in the parish today face the same dilemmas as back at the turn of the twentieth century, with their deliveries being spread over a very wide area. Of course today there are warm vans to travel in, whereas their counterparts a century earlier would have used a bicycle, or if very lucky, a small pony-pulled cart. The double-fronted building to the right of both shots is another of the village's hostelries, the King's Arms. Stane Street, the main road through the village, dissects it from north to south and is of Roman origin.

Weavers Pond on the Green is as pretty today as it was when Percy Lloyd visited it, and it is little wonder that he decided to record it for posterity. In the background to the right of this old photograph we can see the village pump which was given to the village in 1837 by local governess, Jane Scott. The well beneath descends to 70ft and water was lifted by a large iron pump which was sadly removed in the mid-1960s, but has now been thankfully replaced. With a dropping water table in the area, the pump is today little more than a memorial to days gone by.

Ockley has a very successful reputation as a cricketing village and as Percy's final picture clearly shows in the early 1900s, the Green was used to play this magnificent game. The fence surrounding the pitch was supposed to protect it from wandering animals, which at the time were allowed to roam freely. The barrier was, however, no deterrent for the Ockley sheep pictured here. The double-gabled building to the left was the schoolhouse, which opened in 1841 and was again a gift to the village from Miss Jane Scott. In the middle background is St John's Church, which was erected in 1872 and served the villagers until 1983.

Cricket Ground & Cottages, Beare Green.                    Pub. by W. H. Geary, Beare Green.

Our old photograph of the row of the fourteen cottages which over look Beare Green's cricket pitch was published by local postmaster, William Geary. The post office was located to the left of the image across the Newdigate road, which runs from the middle left to the middle background, so Mr Geary would have had a view of these cottages as he went about his daily work. Cricket is no longer played on the Green because of the hazard posed by the busy A24, which fringes its south-western edge. But stoolball is played here during the summer by the Capel club, and they are a force to be reckoned with on the local circuit.

Palmer's Farm, Beare Green.

This traditional local farm located on the Newdigate road just west of Beare Green is believed to date back to about 1550 with seventeenth-century additions. A selection of three barns is built around a central courtyard area with the farmhouse to one side. While the barns today remain, albeit in a slightly less loved condition than the original, the farm is still operational and has not succumbed to becoming small rural business development. Palmers Farmhouse was described to me as having all the charm of an eighteenth-century farm with a modern twist. I have to say that today, given the finances, I would jump at the opportunity to live and work this long-established farm.

Post Office, Beare Green.                    Pub. by W. H. Geary, Beare Green.

William and Lizzie Geary moved to the village in 1906 to take over the post office and general stores from Fred and Michael Dean, the premises being located on the north-eastern edge of the Green. The Deans started the original post office from the shed with double doors to the left of the store. William ran the post office and store until his death in 1951, after which it was run by his daughter until closure five years later. Today the old post office and general store has been split into two private dwellings.

It is hard to image that the quaint little cottage named Noah's Ark was once the home to the Bourne family. Today it lies in the southern side of the front car park of the Duke's Head public house and remains a historic treasure of the area, attracting much attention during the summer months from passers-by. The building is roughly square in shape with a small room in the roof, in which the only way to move around is to stoop.

The Duke's Head at Beare Green has always commanded a prime position on the main road. Even today, with the A24 widened to a dual-carriageway, its position still attracts much passing trade. The pub itself has seen a great deal of change, as can be seen by comparing the old and new views. The new extension to the left of our modern image houses a restaurant which serves traditional Sunday lunches. It has also had a great many landlords over the years, one of the most noteworthy being Mr Wood. He was known locally for producing geese for Christmas, but in 1850 fell foul of thieves (excuse the pun) who stole his entire flock. As the geese would have been fattened for the locals, it must be assumed that the Christmas of 1850 was a miserable one for the people of Beare Green.

# 7
# *The Holmwoods*

The Royal Oak on Chart Lane is known locally as the 'the pub at stone bridge'. This is because of the little stone arched bridge that used to span Bents Brook, which fringes the pub's garden to the south. Indeed even our old picture, which is an advertising card produced for the then landlord H. Payne, refers to it as the Royal Oak Inn, Stone Bridge. The pub has changed a great deal in recent years with the building of a huge dining room and off-road car park in what was a considerably large garden. Comparing the two images we can again say that although the view has changed, it is still easily recognisable and has not lost any of its rustic charm. The Royal Oak remains extremely popular with locals and passing trade (as it is on one of the many short-cut cross-country routes to the south and west of the town) and has an excellent reputation for good food.

ST. JOHN'S CHURCH, & COMMON, NORTH HOLMWOOD.

The village green in North Holmwood with its pretty little pond is situated at the foot of Spook Hill with St John's church overlooking it. Holmwood Common was owned by the Duke of Norfolk until 1956 when he donated it to Dorking Urban District Council. The construction of the church started in August 1874 after North Holmwood became a parish. Today the village boasts one of the only lady vicars in the area. Happily the two views have changed very little with the little pond as popular now with local youngsters as it was in about 1910 – the date of the old photograph.

North Holmwood Village. Underwood's Series

Our old view of the village store, locally known as the cabin (after the original little hut that served the purpose), dates from 12 August 1914. We know this not from a postmark, but because the advertising board displays the newspaper headline 'Britain declares war on Austria' – a landmark day in the history of Great Britain which marked the start of the First World War. In the background is the home of the manager of North Holmwood Brick Company with the road to the right leading to the brickworks itself. The building was extensively altered in 1932 to act as a showcase for the bricks the company produced. The building today has been converted into a number of residential units with little change to its fascia.

It was the commoners' right – as those who lived in the boundary of the common were referred – to graze their animals and fowl on the common and over the village green and this right was exercised for much of the first half of the twentieth century. They were also permitted to cut and collect bracken for animal bedding from August each year. Grazing animals on the green started to become a problem when traffic increased on the main road through the village after the Second World War, and even though the route has been bypassed, you are unlikely to meet a cow face-to-face on the green these days. Comparing the views you will notice that there are still willows on the green, however they are not the originals, which had to be cut down owing to old age in the 1980s. The old photograph was produced for P. Frost, who was the owner of the general stores throughout the 1920s.

Bentsbrook Road takes its name from the small stream which fringes it on the northern side. The houses were built to a very high standard in a 1920s-style design, and even today are highly sought-after for their large room size. In our old view at the end of the road can be seen a set of gates, behind which is a huge pile of what looks like builder's rubble. This could be the start of the development further down the street or just a waste dump for the nearby brickworks. The modern view shows that the eastern end of the road has been fully developed. Even the old village hall, which was located on the right-hand side of the road at the end of the original terrace, has been demolished for housing. As a teenager, the village hall was the venue for many of my Friday evenings as it was the home of Holmwood's Scout troop, the 18th Dorking, with scoutmaster Skip Drakely in charge.

Holmsdale Road (known in 1920 as Brooklyn Terrace) was for many years a cul-de-sac with gates at its eastern end leading into the brickworks which was founded in about 1870. The brickworks operated two kilns with huge smoke stacks, and in its heyday produced many thousands of red bricks a week which were noted for their hardness. The pit closed in the late 1960s while under the ownership of Redlands, who tried wherever possible to re-employ the workers at other sites in the area. At the beginning of the twentieth century, many villagers still owned and worked animals, which would explain the presence of the four cows in the road. The terraced houses remain today, but the cows have been replaced by cars and the brickworks is now the site of a huge Wimpy and Ideal Home estate of modern housing.

FLINT HILL, N. HOLMWOOD. THE SHANTY SERIES.

An old motorised open-top double-decker, probably on the 414 route between Horsham and Croydon, trundles its way up Flint Hill on its journey north into Dorking town centre at around 7.20 p.m. The Windmill public house is obscured by the bus in our old image and sadly in the modern picture is boarded up following its closure. Since the modern view was photographed, the site has been levelled and redeveloped into housing, showing just how quickly things can change. The terrace of old cottages to the left was pulled down in the 1980s and the site developed into flats. The terrace of houses to the right was demolished slightly earlier and today is left as a grassy area. Our modern picture was taken early on a weekend morning as the road is heavily used by traffic at most other times.

On Holmwood Common.                              Pub. by E. Bond, Holmwood.

Another pond, this time at Mid-Holmwood with Bond's village store in the middle background and a horseless open-top carriage outside. The shallow pond was known locally as Bond's pond. It dominates the foreground here, and was used by passing wagons and carts to swell their wheels. In our old picture it is being utilised by the commoners' free-ranging stock for a drink. Today the store has sadly closed and the pond has been dramatically reduced in size as the A24 dual carriageway carves its way through the heart of the common en route to Horsham. The store managed to remain open after the widening of the road, but finally closed it doors to villagers in the late 1970s. Although not visible, the pond is still there, located just below the iron railings in the foreground of the modern picture.

The Norfolk Arms is located at the heart of Mid-Holmwood, just south of the pond on the previous pictures. It was one of two hostelries located almost opposite each other on the main road. The second, known as the Nag's Head, is now also a private residence. The Norfolk Arms has played many roles in the history of this part of Holmwood and it is where a local man Frank Pierce started work as a fly proprietor. He started with carriages and as the age of the motor car came about, the change to motor-driven transport was taken and he established a garage next to the inn in about 1920. The inn's location made it a prime place for local organisations to meet. It played host to the Foresters' Friendly Society; the Working Men's Hunt started from here each Boxing Day and the Annual Holmwood church parade began from the inn on the second Sunday in September. The modern building which replaced the inn is partially hidden behind a high hedge to try to provide some privacy to the residents on this extremely busy section of the A24.

Cricket Ground, South Holmwood.

Village cricket is synonymous with rural life in this part of England and South Holmwood was no exception. Its cricket was played on the Green opposite the Holly and Laurel Inn for over 100 years, but became yet another victim of the devastation created by widening of the A24 at this point in the 1960s. In its heyday, cricket at this venue could command an audience in excess of 2,000 on a good afternoon, attracted by the fine sport and also the teas served from the pub. The local clergy also played a role in Holmwood's cricketing success with vicar, the Revd Edward Wickham, winning honours in its early days, and in latter years the Revd Francis Spurway, who played for the club for nineteen seasons. Regrettably today the cricket team is no more, the public house has disappeared and the A24 has become one of the busiest roads in the area.

Built from money raised by public subscription, the village hall has always been a popular venue for everything from birthday parties and weddings to whist drives and choir practice. Its facilities have included over the years a gymnasium, provision of lunches, a reading room, a billiards table, and with the disappearance of local public houses, it is today the only licensed premises in South Holmwood. With all the development around the village, the hall and club has changed very little externally in over 100 years. Today the club is still popular with the locals and has strong teams playing both darts and pool to a very high local standard.

The Plough, Blackbrook, Holmwood.

Tucked deep in the heart of Holmwood Common, the Plough has offered sustenance to villagers and travellers alike for well over 100 years. For many years it was the luncheon stop for the local Working Men's Hunt on Boxing Day and it isn't difficult to imagine the group milling in the bar exchanging stories of the morning's exploits over beer and sandwiches. In more recent times the pub has become well known locally for its summer hanging baskets and floral displays, which have won numerous prestigious awards. In our modern picture some of these can be seen on the bottom right-hand side of the wall.

# 8

# *Holmbury, Abinger & Wotton*

The geological make-up of the hills around Holmbury is primarily sandstone and this means that during the wet winter months the area remains remarkably dry. At the beginning of the twentieth century this was noted by farmers from as far away as Kent, and with the onset of winter thousands of sheep would arrive with their shepherds by train at Gomshall. Tralee is located on the northern side of the village on the Horsham road running down to Abinger village. It is along this road that the sheep would have been driven at the start of winter and back again in spring. Very little has changed along this road for over 100 years as can clearly been seen when comparing the old and modern views.

For the majority of the twentieth century, Holmbury St Mary's post office, which is located on Pitland Street, was run by the Bullen family. Posted in 1906, our old postcard possibly shows Harry Bullen, the postmaster at the time. Holmbury post office, like so many rural businesses, attracted many visitors and diversified into selling teas, cakes, ice cream and cigarettes. The last recorded postmaster was Godfrey Bullen. Today the building is a private residence which still retains its heritage with a name plaque 'The Old Post Office'.

This old image is again a little misleading as Pitland Street is roughly where the photographer is standing, but the view is north towards the Green, looking down Holmbury Hill Road. One of the three characters pictured in our old image is dressed in a post office uniform and could well be a member of the Bullen family. To the right of both pictures we can see the King's Head public house, which is one of the oldest buildings in the village dating back to before 1839. Behind the pub was once a brewery which served the village and a few additional hostelries. The old stone wall has today been removed to enable patrons to park outside the venue, but externally the pub is still easily recognisable.

Holmbury has developed out of the arrival of the railways to Gomshall in about 1849 and was originally made up of the two independent hamlets of Felday and Pitland Street. Like the vast majority of places, the Green is at the centre of village life and in Holmbury's case is overlooked by the local church and a public house, the Royal Oak. At the time of our old image the house in the centre of the view was the village shop, though today it has become a private residence. To the left of the view is a short lane leading to an opening in the woodland locally known as the Glade, and this is where the village hall is located. Tucked away from main commuter travel, Holmbury is today still a very tranquil place to live or visit.

Abinger Hammer is famous for many things, including the production of watercress in the clear waters of the River Tillingbourne. However, most people remember the village for its clock tower with bell beneath which is stuck on the hour by an animated figure clutching a blacksmith's hammer. A common misconception is that the village gained its name from this character. It is more likely, however, that the valley in which it is located was strongly involved in the iron industry and the name most probably comes from the water-powered trip hammers used for shaping pig iron. The road running through our images is today part of the busy A25 route between Guildford and Dorking.

A view from the eastern side of the village looking west towards the hammer clock (which is just out of view in the right-hand middle background). The white picket fence in the old image surrounds Grasmere, built in 1870 and at one time the village post office. The post office is now located next door to the old building in a house built for William King in about 1881. At the time of writing it has not be subject to potential closure, the fate so sadly inflicted on many rural post offices today. Comparison of the old and new images show that very little has changed in nearly 100 years, other than the addition of white lines to the road.

The River Tillingbourne runs through the heart of Abinger Hammer and splits the Green in two. Spring-fed, the Tillingbourne rises at the foot of Leith Hill, wending its way north-west down through Wotton and Abinger on its way to meet the River Wey just south of Guildford. To the right and slightly behind the camera is the cricket green which was donated to the village by the owners of Abinger Hall in about 1960, in memory of those who lost their lives during the Second World War. Cricket is still played here today, but the village green is probably best known for hosting the annual teddy bears' picnic on the May Day bank holiday every year.

The Tudor farmhouse known as Hatch Farm was built on the site of an older manor house called Harms Hatch. Hatch indicates the existence of a gate across the road, here acting as a parish boundary. Located at the western side of the village of Abinger Hammer, the property falls just inside the Shere parish boundary, possibly confirming this theory. The area from which the modern picture was taken is today a marsh, and obtaining the image was extremely precarious. It is also worth noting that the property has been subject to modern development with an extension to the gable frontage.

Located at the heart of Abinger Common opposite the Norman church of St James is a fine public house called the Abinger Hatch. This charming hostelry has been the sanctuary for many a weary walker as they either ascended or descended the road towards the summit of Leith Hill. Our old image is another fine example of Lloyds of Albury and shows a groomed open carriage awaiting passengers. Opposite the pub on the northern side of the Green are the village stocks, one of only a few locally preserved examples. The village pond is also close by and was most probably located there as a stopping place for carts and carriages. Today the pub is very popular with both local and visiting trade, and boasts some fine cask-conditioned beers together with an excellent menu. Internally it retains the feeling of a good old English pub including oak beams and a log fire in winter.

Readers could be forgiven for thinking that I am obsessed with public houses, but it is a fact that the Mole Valley is blessed with more than its fair share of excellent hostelries. The Volunteer at Sutton Abinger is yet another fine example, located midway between Abinger Common, Abinger Hammer and Holmbury St Mary. Running past the pub is a small rill known locally as the Sutton. Its source is in a field opposite post office corner in the village of Holmbury St Mary and the stream flows northwards to enter the Tillingbourne just east of Abinger Hammer. As can be seen from the comparison between our old and new image, very little has changed in 100 years – even the pillar box is still happily serving residents passing the crossroads here.

The dam in the middle foreground dates from the sixteenth century and was built to create a good head of water to turn the mill wheel of the mill house located to the middle left. This could have been built to mill corn or possibly for use in the gunpowder trade which was prevalent to the west in Albury. It is believed the mill closed in about 1736, but the area was a popular venue for visiting Londoners as transportation developed with train and motor vehicles. As this little hamlet nestles in a steep-sided valley, today's visitors are provided with car parking at the top of the hills on either side and encouraged to walk to visit this area of local beauty.

The Wotton Hatch is an eighteenth-century inn located at the top of Coast Hill, which in the days of horse-drawn transport would weary even the strongest team. Strangely enough it provided stabling for horses in addition to food and refreshment for travellers between Dorking and Guildford. Behind the hostelry to the south stands Wotton House, the home of the Evelyn family. The Evelyn Estate was a vast concern and provided work for many hundreds of people in its heyday. John Evelyn learned the skills of water engineering on a trip to Italy and on his return put these to good practice in the gardens of the house by creating gravity-driven fountains. The Evelyn Estate today still provides work and homes for many local people, although the house has since changed hands on a number of occasions. In its life it has been occupied by the army (during the Second World War), used as a training centre for Surrey Fire Brigade and is now a venue for conferences and seminars. Located on what is now a very busy section of A25, the Wotton Hatch pub still retains a rustic charm as our modern picture demonstrates.

# 9

# Westcott, Leith Hill & Mickleham

The Evelyn family influence reached out to Westcott in the form of a donation of land in 1851 for the construction of Holy Trinity Church. Designed by the famous architect Sir George Gilbert Scott in fourteenth-century Gothic style, the church dominated the entrance to the village from Guildford to the east. The first vicar was the Revd Henry Seymour, who is recorded as having held the position from 1852 to 1864. The church was consecrated the same year as the Revd Mr Seymour took office, with the south aisle and chapel following in 1855. The church's fine clock was added to the steeple in 1887 to mark Queen Victoria's Golden Jubilee and the lych gate was built for her Diamond Jubilee. The church is today sadly partially obscured by trees, but remains the centre of the Church of England portion of Westcott's congregation.

To the western edge of the village stands the lodge marking the entrance to the Rookery which was built on land purchased from Abraham Tucker (owner of Betchworth Castle) by Daniel Malthus in 1759. Malthus constructed a huge dwelling with two mills, a laundry and an ice house which was famous for its heather-thatched roof. The Rookery Mansion exchanged hands a number of times during its life, but sadly was demolished in 1966. Its beautifully landscaped gardens still remain and can be viewed by those who care to venture along the entrance road.

The Crown is the oldest public house in Westcott and has strong association with coaching throughout the eighteenth and nineteenth centuries. To the rear of the property was stabling and a meadow where fresh or additional horses could be obtained for the long struggle up the hill to Wotton and Guildford beyond. It was from this inn that the Court Baron met to determine manorial matters, particularly the use of common fields and the transfer of copyhold land and property. The mere fifty years between our old and new image shows very little has changed other than the inclusion of a footpath necessitating the moving of the pub's sign board.

Westcott is spoilt with three public houses to choose from. The Prince of Wales vies for business with the Crown as the two hostelries lie on almost opposite sides of the road to each other. The Prince of Wales has strong associations with the Tucker family who held the licence for the premises for much of the pub's 150-year history. When the family moved on, they established the local motor repair business of Tucker of Westcott. Our modern image has been captured on a quiet weekend morning, as this scene during weekdays can be far from tranquil with traffic thundering through and dissecting the village in two.

The 64ft tower, which was erected in 1765 by Richard Hull, sits proud at the summit of Leith Hill. The battlements and external staircase were features added a little later to the folly in about 1864. This was a very popular tourist attraction with Victorian and Edwardian visitors – a fact that was exploited by local shopkeeper Henry Roffey, who during the summer months ran a refreshment tent close to the tower. The tower's constructor left instructions in his will that upon his death he should be buried within the tower. His wishes were honoured and the tower is today a tomb to its creator. The effort exerted to reach the top with the additional climb to the viewing platform will reward you with fine views to the South Downs and beyond on a clear day.

W. Parrott.                                    Burford Bridge H

Formerly known as the Fox and Hound, it is alleged that Keats completed his famous poem 'Endymion' here. The Burford Bridge has played host to the rich and famous in its lifetime, many of whom were visiting local celebrity George Meredith, whose famous chalet is a short walk from the hotel. It has over the course of time been developed and extended on many occasions and even boasts a fine tithe barn which was moved from Abinger. Both internally and externally the hotel is still a very luxurious place to visit and stay with the beautiful backdrop of Boxhill and some fantastic walks along the River Mole through the Mole Valley.

Before the construction of the busy A24 dual carriageway, Chalk Pit cottages stood on a narrow winding country lane between Dorking and Leatherhead. The construction work in 1937 saw the development of the route to cater for the increasing traffic demands of the time. The route is still heavily used and is renowned at weekends for its popularity with the motorcycling fraternity. Locally known as the Mickleham Bends, it has been necessary to introduce traffic-calming measures like hatching to help reduce speeding and accidents. Further down the road from this image and on the northbound carriageway, the local authorities have erected a speed camera which sadly has become a popular target for vandalism.

Hidden away on the right-hand side of the picture is the William IV public house and further along the road the National School, which opened in 1843. The road sweeping uphill to the right leads to Bytton Hill Cottages, which command beautiful views over the fields towards Norbury Park. The fine Italian restaurant Frascati can be seen in the middle foreground of our modern picture. This section of road was famous in the past for dining, but of a slightly different cuisine – just north of this picture was a famous 1930s transport café on the route to London!

# ACKNOWLEDGEMENTS

Many people have contributed in so many ways in ensuring this book is published. I would especially like to thank:

William (Bill) Williams – my dad
Alan and Sally Inglis – Melbourne, Florida
Capel Camera Club – without whose contribution this title would not have been possible
Dorking Guides – The cavemen and women who share my passion for local history
Dorking Museum and Dorking Library – who have provided invaluable resources
Mary Day, Beryl Higgins and Jane Lilley for proofreading.

Most of all I would like to thank my little family for supporting me during the tougher times we have had while I was preparing and writing this book.

# BIBLIOGRAPHY

Bennett, Patricia, *Living Stream – Pixham and its People*, Dorking Local History Group, 1994

Bright, J.S., *A History of Dorking and the Neighbouring Parishes*, Simpkin, Marshall & Co., Dorking, 1884

Callcut, John and the Newdigate Society, *The Book of Newdigate: Portrait of a Wealden Village*, Halsgrove, 2002

Ettlinger, Vivien, *Holloway, Dorking: Medieval Farm to Modern Estate*, Dorking Local History Group, 1997

Ettlinger, Vivien, Jackson, Alan A. and Overell, Brian, *Dorking: A Surrey Market Town Through Twenty Centuries*, Dorking Local History Group, 1991

Ferns, Duncan C., *Buckland 1000–2000: A Village History of Buckland, Surrey*, self-published, 1999

Harding, Keith, *Dorking Revisited* Sutton Publishing, 1997

Kohler, Margaret K. (ed.), *Memories of Old Dorking*, Kohler & Coombes, Dorking, 1977

Mercer, Doris and Jackson, Alan A., *Deepdene Dorking*, Dorking Local History Group, 1996

Mitchell, Vic and Smith, Keith, *Country Railway Routes: Guildford to Redhill*, Middleton Press, 1989

Newbery, Celia (ed.), *A History of Sports in Dorking*, Dorking Local History Group and Leith Hill District Preservation Society

Spong, June M., *Around Dorking and Boxhill* Tempus Publishing, 1999

Ryan, Meg and Harding, Keith, *Betchworth in Living Memory*, Goodness Gracious, 2001

Skinner, Julia, *Dorking: A Miscellany – Did you know?*, Francis Frith, 2006

Smith, Bill, *Beare Green & The Holmwoods*, self-published, 1987

Smith, Bill, *A Surrey Village – The Holmwood*, Horsham Press, 1982

Smith, Bill, *A Surrey Village – The Holmwood & District No. 2*, Horsham Press, ND